LIFE SKILLS

Who Makes the World Run?

HERON BOOKS

At Heron Books, we think learning should be engaging and fun. It should be hands-on and it should allow students to move at their own pace.

For this purpose, we have created an accompanying learning guide to help the student progress through this book, chapter by chapter, with increasing confidence, interest and independence.

Get your free learning guide at
heronbooks.com/learningguides.

For a final exam, email
teacherresources@heronbooks.com.

We would love to hear from you!
Email us at *feedback@heronbooks.com.*

Published by
Heron Books, Inc.
20950 SW Rock Creek Road
Sheridan, OR 97378

heronbooks.com

Special thanks to all the teachers and students who
provided feedback instrumental to this edition.

ISBN: 0-89739-104-7

Printed in the USA

22 November 2018

CONTENTS

1 THE TEAM 3

    Introduction 3

    Building Our "Things" 4

    Other Aspects of Life 6

    Your Team..8

2 HOW THE TEAM PLAYS 11

    Simple Basics 12

    Getting Things—Examples 12

    Money 13

    Getting Things—Another Example 14

    Following One's Interest.............................15

    "Wanting" and "Interest" Sometimes Work Together 16

3 FINDING JEANS THAT FIT 21

    The Start of Gap...21

    The (Imaginary) Rest of the Story 22

    Getting Something to Sell 22

    An Overview of the "Team" 28

4 SO YOU HAVE ELECTRICITY AT YOUR HOUSE?...................... 33

Installing Electrical Wires...34

Laws For Electrical Wiring..35

More of the Electrical Wire Team 35

Why Jobs Exist 36

But What About the Electricity? 37

Everybody Plays a Part..38

1

The Team

The Team

INTRODUCTION

For many millions, life in our modern society can be pretty good.

There are things to entertain us, like TV, movies, music, sports and games of all kinds, bicycles to ride, electronic devices to play with or use, concerts to attend, and even places to hike.

There are things that make life much easier than it was for our grandparents or their grandparents, such as cars, nice highways, jet airplane travel, computers, smart phones, the internet, etc.

Modern comforts include air conditioning, food and drink of endless variety, advanced medical care, online shopping with almost anything imaginable shipped to you overnight, and many, many other things that make just "living" much easier and more comfortable.

And no matter what you want to do, there are probably tools (things used to get things done) to help you. For example, there are millions of books to learn from, computer programs to help you do almost anything, and devices of all sorts to help you get things done.

Just to make the point about how many there are, imagine for a moment the life of the "cave man." About the only thing in the list above that was available was "places to hike," and even then there might be a good chance of being killed by some other person or wild animal while out hiking. The point is that in the long time span from then to now, this huge supply of things that make our lives easier has come into existence.

It even can seem that these things are "just there," ready to make our lives more pleasant, and that life consists of using and enjoying them. But how did this enormous supply of nice things come to be?

BUILDING OUR "THINGS"

Step by step, over hundreds of thousands of years, *individual people* have come up with things to improve life.

Maybe it was a better tool, a better way to build a house, a better way to keep food around so you didn't have to hunt all the time, a better way to agree with your fellows not to steal from each other or hurt each other.

Or maybe it was a better way to travel from one place to another, a way to communicate in writing, a way to "catch" or create electrical energy, a way to use electricity to communicate with others, a way to make it safer to go on a hike, and so forth.

Each time someone took a step that improved life, they made it possible for someone else to discover another step that improved life a little more.

Of course there are thousands of examples of this. And trying to imagine all the small and large improvement steps for all those examples is enough to make your head spin!

Just think about the bicycle for a moment. How did we get to have bicycles? Here's a list of just a *few* of the steps.

1. Somebody wanted to move something heavy and had the idea that with a round object under it, an item could be moved more easily by pushing it and letting the round object roll under it.

2. People made better and better round objects.

3. A wheel is a round object, but it isn't a wheel until it has an axle in the middle that holds still while the wheel turns. Someone had the bright idea

that an axle in the middle of a round object really made it more useful, and a simple axle was invented (the birth of the wheel).

4. The axle didn't work very well, and someone thought of a way to make it better. (Already we have probably skipped hundreds or thousands of steps in between.)

5. Someone put two wheels on the same axle with a box in between and made a two-wheeled cart that didn't fall over all the time, the way a one-wheeled cart did.

   (Meanwhile someone else got the idea of catching a big animal and training it to pull the cart, but that's a different story with its own steps.)

6. Someone put two axles under a big box, one at either end, and made a wagon with four wheels (and someone figured out how to make it steerable).

7. At this point something even stranger happens. Someone decided to hook one wheel in front of another and see if it could be ridden down a little hill without falling over. Maybe it was a game, maybe it was serious—it doesn't matter. This person had just created the first ancestor of the modern bicycle!

8. Since a rider couldn't just go downhill all the time, someone had the idea of putting a crank on one wheel so the vehicle could be powered by foot. (We just left out all the steps required to get cranks to work well.)

9. Tired of being shaken to pieces on these contraptions with their hard wheels, someone invented rubber tires. (Imagine how many steps that took!)

10. Tired of running into barns, haystacks, ditches or other people in order to stop, someone invented brakes. They didn't work very well, but they were better than just crashing.

11. Someone figured out better brakes.

12. Since it didn't work very well to have the crank on the wheel, someone got the idea of using a chain (many, many more steps) and little wheels with teeth on them to work with the chain, so the crank could be located more comfortably in between the wheels.

13. Now we have arrived up to about the year 1880. You can just imagine the number of steps of improvement that have happened since then to get to a modern mountain bike or racing bike. If you look up "History of the Bicycle" online, you can see some pictures of a few of the things we have talked about.

That was a very short version of a very long story with more steps in it than would be easy to count. Even if some of the people involved did several steps, the story surely involves thousands and thousands of people all working more or less on the same project, even if they didn't think of it that way. They were each just "doing their thing," but in fact they were cooperating (working together) in the creation of today's bike.

And that was just one item of modern life, the bicycle. Think for a moment about the people involved in development of the airplane. A smart phone. An electric car. And on and on.

OTHER ASPECTS OF LIFE

It isn't just *things* that got developed. Let's go back to the idea of a hike for a moment. Imagine back to times when people lived in small groups. Now imagine the different groups were somewhat hostile, attacking and fighting each other. Perhaps most of the people actually wanted to live peacefully, but some preferred to live by violence and stealing. (This kind of thing is a pretty common story in the history of humankind.)

In an environment like that, you can imagine that taking a hike was a pretty risky business. How did it get to the way it is now, where hikes are pretty safe from violent groups of people wanting to whack you over the head and take your stuff?

The development of what we today call law and order, and a fairly safe environment (including respect for other people's lives and belongings), is a *big* improvement.

Getting as far as we have toward creating a safer environment is such a huge development that it makes the development of the bicycle look pretty simple in comparison. In other words, the development of law and order has involved the help of many more people than the bicycle did, and over huge territories of the earth. You could spend years just trying to list these steps and it would still be incomplete. But here are a few, just for illustration.

1. An agreement among people that what a person created, caught or grew belonged to him or her personally, to control as desired by that person. (This is such a difficult development to achieve that lots of people on earth even now don't have this agreement.) Just imagine the number of people that have worked to get such an agreement among people.

2. The idea of writing down laws so that everyone can be treated the same, instead of people just making up rules as they go along. You could almost tell the story of humankind by just talking about the different sets of laws (often referred to as "codes of law") that have been made up to try to establish law and order.

    These ideas and codes were created by individuals or groups cooperating with each other, working together to solve some situation where people weren't getting along. Often individuals and groups worked to improve rules other groups had tried earlier. In a way, these later groups were cooperating with groups that had tried to solve similar problems at an earlier time and often in a different part of the world.

3. Having judges who could be impartial (fair, not choosing sides) in settling disputes, crimes and punishments was an important development. It meant that the judges didn't have something to gain for themselves by deciding one way or the other. They could be fair to both sides. Good people the world over have worked on this for a very long time, and are still working on it. Some places have it and some do not.

4.   And so on.

Take a moment and consider the number of people working, one way or another, to bring these improvements to humankind. Without those people, it might still be dangerous to take that hike. And a lot of other things would also be very dangerous.

Getting law and order and a safe environment is something we all want. But, like other things, it has to be created step by step by good people having ideas and making improvements, one step (or a few steps) at a time.

These are examples of improvements to life that aren't just things or objects. Many, many such examples exist. Consider music and what a huge collection of ideas about music have been developed and collected over the years. The list of these sorts of improvements and developments is probably as long as the list of things or objects that have been developed.

YOUR TEAM

We have barely scratched the surface of this subject, but the overall point is that we have the lifestyle we have today as a result of the contributions over a *long* period of time by an *enormous* number of people. All of this huge collection of tools, comforts, protections, ideas, rights, freedoms and ways of doing things that these people have helped bring about is what we call our *culture*.

The poet Robert Frost said in a beautiful short poem "The Tuft of Flowers":

> "'Men work together," I told him from the heart,
> "Whether they work together or apart."

Whether its members know it or not, humankind is a team that has put together the cultures we have.

Perhaps you hadn't thought about it before, but this is *your* team. You are already on this team, and you will benefit from it and no doubt you will contribute to it as you move on with your life.

2

How The Team Plays

How The Team Plays 2

When we think of humankind as a "team" that has, over a long span of time, developed or evolved what we call our culture, it is perhaps natural to ask, "Why?" or "How did that happen?" Did someone get them all together and agree on a plan? Of course that's a silly question, but it is fairly clear that there was *some sort* of cooperation among the members of humankind over those thousands of years, whether it was planned or not.

For instance, in all the long line of steps in the invention and development of the computer, individuals used the discoveries of those who went before them. This is a kind of cooperation, even if it is not really *together*.

Also, if people wanted to sell their computers, they had to pay attention to what people wanted to buy. This is another kind of cooperation between people.

And suppose a person needed a special tool to build a new version of the computer, and someone somewhere else made such tools. If the computer developer gets the tool from the tool developer, they are cooperating, although they likely don't know each other at all.

If the computer developer got some help from a scientific theory worked out 100 years ago, there was a kind of cooperation between the person working now and the scientist of 100 years ago. After all, cooperation means *co-operation*, or "working together." Even if these people are not physically together, there is a connection between them that affects the actions of one or both of them.

It is because of this kind of cooperation in its millions of ways that we can think of mankind as a kind of "team." Let's dig a little deeper into how this team "plays," how it works and *why* it works.

SIMPLE BASICS

We start off by getting simple—there are two basic ideas that can help explain why the team works:

1. *People want things—they have always wanted things.* For instance, maybe they wanted a better club to whack wild animals with, or they wanted a house instead of a cave. Maybe they wanted a better sailing ship or a good plow horse. Maybe they wanted to hear an orchestra play the new Beethoven music. Maybe now they want a hamburger or a pair of pants. Maybe they want a trip to Antarctica or guitar lessons. Maybe they want the latest cell phone or a new carpet.

2. *People like to do things that interest them.* Maybe something interests them because they are curious and want to learn. Maybe they are interested in helping others. Maybe they are just interested in entertaining themselves by doing some particular thing. People are interested in lots of different things and activities.

As we will see with some examples, each of these ideas by itself helps explain a large part of how and why the team works. And often these two ideas can work together at the same time, and that makes the team even better.

GETTING THINGS—EXAMPLES

Let's look at the first basic. A person, let's call him Bill, wants something. Bill looks around and sees that another person, let's say Joe, can give it to him or help him get it. Bill wants something. Joe can help him get it. Bill figures out something that he can give Joe so that he can get what he wants.

This leads to examples like these:

- A person who is a farmer can raise plants or animals, and trade those products with someone else to get something needed: a better plow horse.

- A person who likes driving can carry people around in a ride service, such as Uber, and use the money from customers to buy things.

- A person who wants a certain car could do handyman work for the family that owns the car (but doesn't need it) until it's been earned.

What we are talking about here is "trading things or services." Giving something and getting something back for it is called **exchange.** We will assume here that we are talking about people with good intentions. That means, among other things, that they aren't trying to steal things of value from other people or trying to trick them into giving good things in return for bad things. Such people want fair exchange, not unfair exchange or dishonest exchange.

Looking at the first example above, suppose the farmer has a large hay crop and someone who raises horses has a good plow horse that she doesn't need, but she does need a supply of hay. If they make the trade, *both of them feel they have gained.* Each felt it was a benefit and made the trade. They weren't particularly *trying* to help each other, they just both got something they wanted by cooperating. The same thing happened in the other two examples. Both sides were happy with the exchanges.

In these examples, we have people cooperating to make things better for everybody involved. Even though they may really only be interested in helping themselves, the exchanges they make are fair and honest, and everyone is happy with the exchange.

But the second example, as you might have noticed, was a little different. The people involved weren't just trading something for something else. The trade made between the driver and the customers involved money, so let's take a brief look at money.

MONEY

Money is something that can go in the middle of trades. It *goes between* people who are exchanging with each other. It is a very smart idea that makes real-life trading much easier.

Suppose the fellow who needs a car to drive people around in knows how to make pencils. He wants to trade pencils for a car. It is pretty unlikely that he will find someone with a car who wants enough pencils to trade for a car.

Money comes to the rescue. Money is something that people agree represents value—it is the *agreement* that makes money work. If people *agree* that money is valuable, they will trade for it.

So in our example, the pencil-maker trades a lot of pencils to a lot of different people, each trade getting a certain amount of money. Perhaps after 5,000 pencils have been made and traded, there is enough money to trade it for the car. The person is still basically trading pencils for the car—money just allows the trade to be broken down into a lot of smaller parts.

Money is such a useful idea that most of the trades we see in life are trading some object or service for money. Then sooner or later the person who got the money trades it for something else. So the basic action is still *people trading goods or services for other goods or services*. It's just that nowadays there is almost always money in between.

The important thing for our discussion here is that people make these trades because they want something for themselves or their family, friends or groups. They are trying to improve something for themselves. But even though they're doing it for themselves, it leads to a kind of teamwork that improves the lives of all the people involved.

GETTING THINGS—ANOTHER EXAMPLE

The development of the computer is one of the most obvious changes of recent times, and as discussed, thousands of small and large steps were involved in getting from "no computer" to today's computers. Probably just about every one of these steps happened as a trade. Let's look at how this has worked (and is still working today).

1. A company wants to sell computers to lots of people (trade them for money that the company can use to trade for things it needs or wants).

2. The company figures out what improvement would get people interested in trading money for the company's computers.

3. The company hires computer expert Molly (trades money to her for her work) to help them invent such an improvement.

4. The company has other workers manufacture the computers (trades money with them for the work).

5. The company trades the computers with many individual people for a lot of money.

6. Now the world has an improved computer available to it. And in the process the company has money to do something else with, and lots of people have computers.

7. Another computer company does the same steps but for a different kind of improvement.

8. And another computer company does the same, and another computer company does the same, and so on.

And the world keeps getting better computers. After this goes on for 50 years, the world has gone from "no computer" to what we have today. This is what the "team" has produced, even if at each step everyone just wanted to get something for themselves.

So the first basic point is simple: people want things and they will trade to get them. The result is improvements, and everybody gains something.

FOLLOWING ONE'S INTEREST

Let's look now at the second basic point. When good people follow their own interests, it doesn't always help other people, but it isn't harmful to others. They might just be entertaining themselves in a way that doesn't affect others, but very often such people take pleasure in doing things that they enjoy and that *also* help others in some way.

For example, suppose a person is interested in growing strawberries—just likes strawberries and everything about them, and works with them as a hobby. Suppose that person also gets interested in seeing if it's possible to breed a kind of strawberry that is not harmed by certain bugs and that still tastes good. This is just a game of interest to this individual, but if successful, will benefit others—both from what is learned in plant breeding and from having this new kind of strawberry around.

As another made-up example, suppose a medical researcher inherits a lot of money and doesn't really need to earn any money to live well, but has a personal interest in finding a cure for the disease diabetes. Perhaps there is a relative with diabetes, or something else sparked an interest. For whatever reason, this individual sets out to research and experiment on ways to help people with diabetes. Maybe it's successful, maybe it isn't—maybe at least the data from the research helps others who are working on the same cure. Either way, many people are helped.

These two examples (and many more you could make up) show how the team can be helped even when the person didn't get anything for it. (Actually, they probably *would* get something for it—such as recognition and appreciation for their work, but that is probably not why they did it.)

"WANTING" AND "INTEREST" SOMETIMES WORK TOGETHER

Something that can make the team much more powerful in achieving improvements is when the two basic points work together. A person wants things, *and* also enjoys doing what helps get those things. People generally want things—food and a home for their family, a car, music lessons or whatever— and so they have to do *something* productive or creative in order to exchange for what they want.

People are often very fortunate to find that their *interest* steps in to help them at this point. In other words, it frequently turns out that they can do something they are interested in *and* produce or create something they can exchange. This makes the "team" work even better.

Someone is interested in building nice furniture and from the furniture building can buy a car. Someone who likes messing around with electronics builds a new gadget that people want, and as a result can afford to take a trip around the world. It is the best of possibilities—these persons got to do something they were interested in. As a result they got to have something they wanted, *but also* other people in the world benefitted by getting better furniture or a new helpful electronic gadget, etc.

These various kinds of teamwork are very powerful. They have brought humankind from cave man to today's world of comfort, health and pleasure. Most of us don't notice this teamwork. It just happens, with most of humankind participating, even when they don't think of it that way.

Economists (people who study exchange and all the back-and-forth of things, services and money in society) sometimes call this teamwork the "unseen hand." This is an imaginative way of describing the fact that people who are really just "doing their own thing" and working for their own benefit just naturally end up cooperating and exchanging with other people who are really just "doing their own thing."

It is as though some guiding force (the "unseen hand") is steering things in a good direction. In other words, it is just another way of describing the natural cooperation of this "team" that we have been looking at. In a way, there can seem to be something magical or invisible about it, and the "unseen hand" is just an effort to describe that.

We all benefit from this teamwork, and if we can imagine and describe it as the "unseen hand," we can also imagine grabbing and holding tightly to it—after all, it is what keeps the world running.

3

Finding Jeans That Fit

Finding Jeans That Fit

3

If you have ever been glad to find a store that provides *just* what you were looking for, you know how nice that can be. But what if that store had not existed? And how do such stores come into existence? Let's take a look in some detail at a real example.

Doris and Don Fisher opened Gap, Incorporated[1] in 1969 as a single store in San Francisco. According to the Gap website, Don was frustrated because he found it very difficult to buy Levi jeans that fit him well. He and Doris were experienced in business. They had worked with Don's father in a cabinet-making business and also had their own business of buying and renovating old hotels.

THE START OF GAP

Doris and Don felt that selling jeans and pants could be a fast-growing business, because other people probably had the same sort of frustration Don was experiencing. Eventually they decided to open their own store which would specialize in selling Levi jeans to customers in the 12–25 year-old age group. It would offer all the styles, colors and sizes that Levi Strauss and Company made.

According to the Gap website, Don said, "I created Gap with a simple idea: to make it easier to find a pair of jeans." They also planned to sell music in the form of records and tapes. (Neither CDs nor digital downloads existed in 1969.)

---

1   *Incorporated* or *Inc.* after a company's name means that the company was formed according to certain laws. Companies formed this way are called *corporations*. Many large and small companies are corporations.

Doris and Don were "entrepreneurs." An *entrepreneur* is someone who has an idea for a business and either starts it himself or provides money for others to get it going. Entrepreneurs usually have a lot of creativity, courage or money, or some combination of these qualities. There are risks and costs involved in starting a new business. Doris and Don Fisher had some of all the above qualities and they were willing to risk their money and time to create and run this new type of clothing store.

Their risk, and a lot of hard work, paid off. After 19 years, there were over 3,000 Gap stores with combined sales of over $14 billion per year! What Don decided to do, he definitely achieved. He made it a lot easier for a lot of people to find a pair of jeans! It is a good example of how following one's own interest can benefit not only oneself, but also many others.

THE (IMAGINARY) REST OF THE STORY

A lot must have happened in those 19 years, and obviously it wasn't all done by Don and Doris.

Even though many of the following things *may* have happened as they are described here, none of what follows is based on actual facts (except for the details about the actual store). We're just imagining the kinds of things that probably happened. Since it is imaginary, we will start referring to the people starting the company as "the owners," and give some of the other people made-up names.

GETTING SOMETHING TO SELL

After they had the idea of opening Gap, the owners contacted Levi Strauss and Company (we'll now just call them "Levi Strauss") to work out how to buy lots of jeans of all styles, colors and sizes, so they could sell the jeans in their store.

After some meetings, the owners and Levi Strauss signed a contract. A *contract* is an agreement, usually in writing, that a person or company must keep. Even if one side of the agreement later on doesn't want to keep the agreement, they can be made by law to keep it. In this case, Levi Strauss agreed to provide a certain number and types of jeans to the owners, and the owners agreed to pay a certain price for each pair they bought.

The contract was important to the owners because if they risked their time and money opening the Gap, they had to depend on Levi Strauss to provide them with jeans at a certain price. If after two months Levi Strauss said, "We can't sell you jeans anymore," then the Gap would have gone out of business. The contract was also important to Levi Strauss because if they started making more jeans for Gap but later Gap refused to buy them, then Levi Strauss could lose a lot of money.

Setting Up the Business

The owners hired a lawyer, Will Gransome, to help them with the contract. A *lawyer* is someone well educated in laws. A company the size of Levi Strauss has a team of lawyers, so between Gap's lawyer and the Levi Strauss' team of lawyers, all the details of the contract were worked out to the satisfaction of both companies. The owners' lawyer also helped them with other laws they needed to know about to start up their company.

After the owners knew that they could get the jeans (and music—probably making similar agreements) they needed, they had to find a building for their store. They started looking for a building, but soon realized that they didn't have the time or the knowledge to find what they were looking for.

So, they hired Kathie MacGruder, a real estate agent. *Real estate* means "land and the buildings on it." An *agent* is a person hired to act for someone else. *Real estate agents* are people hired by individuals or companies to help them buy, sell or rent land, buildings, homes, office space, etc.

The owners told Kathie that they wanted to rent a building for a clothing store. Kathie helped them work out exactly what they were looking for: the size of the building, what sort of area in the city they wanted to be in, and how much they could afford to pay. The owners wanted a building in an area where there were lots of people ages 12 to 25 and where there was plenty of parking available.

Kathie helped them locate several buildings that seemed to match what they were looking for. She then went with them to visit all the buildings on the list. The owners liked a certain building on Ocean Street in San Francisco.

Kathie arranged a meeting between the owners and the building's owner to discuss arrangements for renting the building. Will Gransome was brought in to review the rental contract in which the owners agreed to pay a certain amount each month, and the building owner agreed to rent the building to them for a certain number of years. The contract also listed out agreements about what changes the owners could or could not make to the building (remodeling it and painting it, etc.).

The owners now needed to remodel the building to make it attractive and suitable for a clothing store. They wanted a building that would not only catch the eye of young people but would be set up well as a clothing store.

As you may have guessed, by this time the owners began to need some additional money. This is why an entrepreneur either needs to have or get money to start up a business. They had already hired the lawyer, Will Gransome, and the real estate agent, Kathie MacGruder, even though the business wasn't earning any money yet. So far they had been paying all the expenses from their savings. The cost of remodeling the building was more than they could afford.

They decided to find a bank that would loan them some money. They went to their local bank and explained that they needed a loan to pay for remodeling the building. A bank makes most of its money by lending money to people or to businesses. When the loan is paid back to the bank, the borrowers pay back more money than was lent to them. That extra amount paid back is how the bank makes its money.

At the bank they talked to a loan officer by the name of Alfredo Ossino. **Loan officers** are employees of the bank who help people work out the details of their loans from the bank. They help customers who want to borrow money, and they make sure that whoever they lend money to will actually pay it back.

The loan officer and the owners discussed the loan, how much it would be, how much per month they would have to pay the bank, etc. Then they signed a loan agreement—another contract. With this money the owners were now ready to get started on remodeling the building.

Because they wanted their building to be attractive and efficient, they hired an architect and an interior designer. **Architects** and **interior designers** plan how the outside of buildings will look, how the inside parts of the building will look and be organized, and the colors, furniture and lighting. The architect and the interior designer worked with the owners to decide what the plans would look like and then to draw up the plans.

After the plans were drawn, the owners needed a building contractor, usually called a contractor, to do the actual remodeling of their building. A **contractor** is someone who signs a contract to do some work for a certain price.

The contractor agreed to remodel their building in exchange for a certain amount of money. The remodeling involved ripping out some of the old walls and building new ones. It involved adding new and bigger windows so people walking by could see inside and get interested in buying jeans and music. Shelves were built, storage spaces created, small office spaces added, new light fixtures and carpeting installed, dressing rooms and more rest rooms built and the entire building inside and out painted in bright colors. (You can go to the Gap, Inc. website and click "About Gap, Inc." to see a photograph of the original Gap store and its colorful exterior on Ocean Avenue in San Francisco.)

To get this work done the contractor hired carpenters, electricians, carpet layers, painters and others. And they in turn worked with many different stores and businesses to get the supplies, like lumber, wire, paint, carpet, etc.

Getting Customers

At about this point the owners realized that they needed to start advertising so that when they opened their store, there would be customers who knew they were there and who might be ready to start buying jeans and music. They realized that if they opened the store but had not started advertising, they might not have many customers for a few weeks.

They needed to have plenty of customers as soon as the store opened because they knew they would have expenses to pay (such as payments for rent, electricity, telephone, wages for employees, jeans from Levi Strauss, music from music companies, bank loan payments, lawyers' fees, architect and interior designer fees, advertising costs and so on).

Because they didn't want to waste their money with ineffective advertising, they looked for help from people who were expert at it. They found an advertising company that had a good record of helping other companies get more customers.

The advertising company was run by a manager, Marie Mathews, who coordinated the activities of her employees. The owners met with Marie and Peter St. George, the advertising art director, to discuss what kind of advertising they wanted. An **advertising art director** is responsible for producing new ideas for advertising of all kinds, like television, internet, posters, billboards, magazines, etc. Peter worked with a **researcher** who had statistics showing that people ages 12 to 25, who wear Levis and like to buy music, tend to read a certain type of magazine. Peter brought in artists, writers and photographers, and they worked as a team to create a plan with sketches of possible magazine advertisements.

When the owners agreed on a plan, Peter hired a modeling agency to get models to wear the clothes for photographs for the ads. For several days Marie and Peter worked with models, photographers and makeup artists while hundreds of photographs were taken of the models wearing different kinds of Levis. Later Peter and his employees put the photographs together into the actual advertisements and took them to the offices of various magazines to talk to the advertising directors of the magazines.

Magazines make money by selling magazines. But they often make more of their money by charging other companies who want to advertise in the magazine. **Advertising directors** are responsible for getting enough advertisements into the magazines and for helping to ensure that the advertisements are successful so that more and more companies want to advertise in that magazine. Peter selected several magazines for the clothing store advertisements, and arranged for them to be paid.

Up and Running

Meanwhile on Ocean Avenue, the owners had interviewed 50 people who applied for work at their store. Nine people were hired: six salespersons, a warehouse worker (to unload and store the boxes of Levis and music and to keep the shelves stocked), a janitor, and an office worker (to answer the phone and keep track of the money and paperwork).

One of the owners acted as the store manager, supervising the other employees and seeing that the customers got good, fast service. The other owner was responsible for doing everything to keep the store open and able to sell. That included ordering more Levis and music; getting the money into the bank; paying all the bills; staying in touch with the advertising art director to keep the advertising effective, and so on.

Gap, Incorporated held a grand opening party, planned by the advertising art director Peter St. George. The store was decorated with lots of balloons and colorful posters, and customers were given free cake and soda. The top disc jockey from KEWB, the popular San Francisco rock 'n roll radio station was there and a local rock band played in front of the store. For the first weekend all jeans were marked "20 percent off!" Sales were great.

The owners stayed in touch with Peter, and after a few weeks, Peter recommended some changes in the advertising plan. Big billboards with models wearing clothes from Gap were put up near movie theaters, concert halls, high schools and colleges. They reduced the number of magazine ads but began some radio and television advertisements.

Six months after the Gap opened, they were selling more jeans and music than they had imagined! Now they had 35 employees. Surveys done by the advertising company showed that over 30% of Gap customers were young people coming from San Jose, a city about one hour south of San Francisco.

Therefore, the owners decided to open another store in San Jose. To do that, they began contacting people to help them again: a real estate agent, lawyer, loan officer, and so on.

AN OVERVIEW OF THE "TEAM"

You can see in our imagined story above that in order to buy a simple pair of jeans from Gap, it was necessary to have many steps of cooperation between many people. Without all those steps of cooperation, the Fishers would not have been able to sell those jeans.

Below is a somewhat more complete but still partial listing of the sorts of people involved in this cooperation—we might think of them as the "Gap team."

Something to remember as you look through this list—most of these folks weren't formally part of any "Gap team"—they didn't start out with some big plan to build Gap, but rather were just pursuing their own lives and interests.

This kind of cooperation arises among people because they all get some satisfaction or benefit from the activity. Perhaps they are participating in order to get money to acquire things they want, or are just doing these things because they were interested in them for one reason or another. It is how the world works.

- entrepreneurs
- people who make jeans
- owners and managers of the jeans company
- people who make records and tapes of music
- lawyers
- real estate agents
- owners of buildings
- loan officers

- architects
- interior designers
- contractors
- carpenters
- electricians
- carpet layers
- painters
- advertising company managers
- advertising art directors
- advertising researchers
- artists
- advertising writers
- photographers
- modeling agency owners and managers
- models
- makeup artists
- magazine advertising directors
- salespersons
- warehouse workers
- janitors
- office workers
- disc jockeys
- rock bands

And guess what? The list above leaves out lots of people. This "team" is surrounded by other "teams" that help them by exchanging needed products or services with them.

For example, people built a clean water system to provide drinking water for San Francisco and to transport that water hundreds of miles to every building in San Francisco. People built a sewer system to take away dirty water and keep it from polluting the buildings in San Francisco.

Who produced all the food eaten in San Francisco every day? Who transported the food from the farms and places that package food to the grocery stores in San Francisco? Who built the refrigerators that kept the food from spoiling and the ovens that cooked the food?

The list goes on and on. There are these sorts of "teams" everywhere.

4

So You Have Electricity At Your House?

So You Have Electricity At Your House?

Imagine for a moment that the electricity to your house was turned off, and it wasn't just temporary, but gone for good, or at least for a very long time. You may have experienced a brief power outage before and been forced to think about this, but even if you have, let's take a very brief look at the first hour or so of a day, and list a few of the things you might use that probably depend on electricity:

- temperature in your bedroom

- alarm clock

- lights

- warm/hot water

- hair dryer

- hot breakfast food

- cold breakfast food

- fresh fruit or other food refrigerated to keep it from spoiling

- toast

- music

- computer

- phone

- garage door

- etc.

Of course some of these can be supplied by other means than electricity, but many cannot. It is pretty easy to see that lack of electricity would make even the first hour of your day quite a bit less comfortable.

So, we can be glad we have electricity, right? But let's stop and ask a few questions about it, such as "What's going on *behind* those wall plugs?" or "Why do we have electricity available here? Where does it come from? How does it get here?"

The answers to these questions lead us to a whole new "team" of people who are getting electricity to your home, school and other places you go.

INSTALLING ELECTRICAL WIRES

Let's start with the electrician who put all the electrical wires in your house. The job of putting in electrical wires is called wiring, and one of the main things an electrician does is wire buildings and homes when they are being built.

It's pretty obvious that by wiring your house (or apartment building), the electrician did something that helped you. But, if you think about it, it would be quite possible to do a very sloppy job of wiring a house, so that the wiring would cause various problems, such as failing to carry electricity properly or causing a fire.

Did your electrician do a good job just because he was a good guy? Well, maybe, but there is more to the story than that.

Some earlier electricians came up with wiring rules to make their wiring safer and more desirable—they wanted to make sure they had a good reputation and would get hired. They were doing this to help themselves get work, but by doing this they did something that helped you (and the rest of us).

LAWS FOR ELECTRICAL WIRING

But a set of rules like this might not be the same in different places, and some rules might not be as good as others. Wouldn't it be better for all of us if there was a really firm set of good rules that was used everywhere?

That's exactly what happened when lawmakers got involved. In order to keep *their* jobs and help the people who voted for them, lawmakers collected up all the best information on wiring and made official laws and rules for how wiring should be done. Then they required all electricians to learn them and follow them.

So, besides the electricians, the lawmakers are another group that helped make your electricity available (and safe).

MORE OF THE ELECTRICAL WIRE TEAM

Up to here, we have discussed only house wiring, and we haven't even discussed all the folks that made the wires available, such as:

- the people (miners) who dig up the rock with copper in it
- the people (refiners) who do the job of getting the small amounts of copper out of the huge amounts of rock
- the people who make the wires
- the people who transport the wires (by train, by truck, by jet, by ship)
- the people who sell the wires

These people are also part of your "get-electricity" team, and they are definitely providing you a service, even if they think they are just earning a living.

WHY JOBS EXIST

Everybody we have talked about (and everybody we will talk about) are "just doing their jobs," which is a very simple way to put it.

But why do these jobs exist?

Every job exists because *someone* wants the product or result of that job, and is willing to trade (or exchange) something for it. In other words, jobs exist because both sides get what they want. The person doing the job gets something (usually money), and the person who wanted the product or result gets something (the product or result he or she paid for).

Consider the job of one of the miners mentioned above. Through many, many steps in between, you or your family traded with the miner. The miner got something wanted (probably money) and you got wiring in your house.

Jobs and exchanges like these lead to the creation of things and ideas that people want, and these new or better things and ideas add improvements to our culture.

That's the way it works. Everybody contributes something—by producing something a person can exchange with others. And in a way, we all also contribute by wanting the things others create.

As a result of all these millions and millions of exchanges back and forth, both the creators and the users are helped, society gets stronger and the culture gradually develops.

We have come a long, long way from cave man days.

BUT WHAT ABOUT THE ELECTRICITY?

Once a house or building has been wired, it still doesn't have electricity until someone brings electricity to that wiring. Where does it come from and how does that happen?

The electrical energy that comes to your house is created at places called power plants. There are different kinds of power plants. Some burn coal or oil to make electricity. Some use flowing water or wind to make electricity. Some use the heat from the sun or from hot water deep in the ground. And some, called nuclear power plants, use energy contained in uranium atoms to create electrical energy. A lot of different jobs are involved in all these kinds of power plants.

Let's pick just one example of a plant—a power plant at a dam on a river that converts the energy from the flowing water into electricity.

Building a dam on a river is a huge job (or collection of jobs):

- Someone has to investigate the rock formations around the river to make sure the dam can be safely built

- Someone has to calculate if there is enough power in the river to create as much electricity as will be needed

- Somebody has to design the dam to ensure it will hold back the rushing water safely

And there are many, many more jobs to help get a dam built.

How about the machinery that the water goes through to make the electricity? This involves another big team even before this dam gets started:

- All the past scientists and workers who figured out how electricity works and designed machines that will turn other forms of energy into electricity

- All the people who manufacture the machinery that turns the flow of water into electricity

- All the people who sell, transport and install the machinery

This is clearly becoming a really big team.

But the electricity still hasn't gotten to your house yet!

It might have to travel hundreds of miles to get there from the power plant. Then it has to be distributed to the buildings in your town. You can imagine that stringing wires across the country takes a lot of people doing a lot of work. Add them to your team.

In your town there is a company called a power company or an electrical company that has traded with all these earlier people to get electricity to your town. And now the power company is ready to trade with you. They hook up the lines to your house and suddenly you have electricity!

The power company keeps track of how much electricity you use each month and then they send you a bill for it. They have supplied something very valuable to you, and you exchange with them for it.

EVERYBODY PLAYS A PART

Have you ever looked closely at a beautiful, detailed spider web? It has many lines connecting in many, many patterns. That's sort of how this huge collection of cooperating people works. There are all these lines of exchange, all connected in a complicated pattern.

So we could call this team a big "web of cooperation."

All these people, whether they exactly mean to or not, are cooperating with each other and you to bring electricity to you (and the rest of us).

And remember, this discussion was just about your electricity. Take a moment and think of other things you depend on, for instance, fresh meat or vegetables, schools, automobiles, movies, police protection, and on and on. Each one has a similar "web of cooperation."

Life goes on, with things to entertain us, things to keep us safe and comfortable, things to help us learn and do things—things almost beyond our imagination. All of these things just seem to "be there" for us, as long as we can afford to pay for them. In fact, there are *so many* of these products and services *so easily* available to us that we often don't even think about how lucky we are.

But it isn't just luck. We happen to be living as part of a big team, each of us doing things to help ourselves and those we care about, but each of us exchanging *something* with others. And everybody benefits.

It all adds up to our culture.

Take a moment every once in a while to think of all the other people on your team. It's really quite an amazing team, isn't it?